Coloring Your Way to a Great Big Smile!

50 Fall Coloring Activities for Mindful Little Ones

Season of Gratitude

Written by Ana Cybela
Illustrated by Widya Arumba

An imprint of Kinetic Dandelions

Copyright ©2020 by Little Dandelions LLC

www.kineticdandelions.com.

All rights reserved. No part of this publication may be reproduced, stored in a retrieval system, or transmitted in any form or by any means, electronic, mechanical, photocopying, recording, or otherwise, without the prior written permission of the publisher.

ISBN: 978-1-7355694-2-0

Recommended for age 3 and up

This Fall Coloring Book Belongs To Mindful

....

Go outside and find a leaf. What color is it?

Look up at the sky. Do you see a bird? Can you hear it?

Jump in a pile of leaves!

Go outside and make friends with a squirrel.

Draw a ladybug!

Blow on a dandelion and make a wish. Watch the tiny seeds fly away.
One, two, three...

Let's go camping!

Hug a pumpkin!

Find some rocks by a creek. Arrange them in any shapes that you like!

Pick some apples!

Bake apple chips!

Make an apple pie!

Make an apple stamp!

Time for a picnic!

Carve a pumpkin!

Roast some pumpkin seeds! Yum!

Time to decorate!

Collect acorns and make art!

Paint a pumpkin!

Enjoy a cup of hot cocoa!

Find some leaves outside and glue them to a window!

Find some birds in the sky. Where are they flying to?

On a rainy day, open a window. Watch, listen, and smell.

Make art with leaves!

Time for an apple cider tea party!

Time to dress up!

Light up a pumpkin!

Try face painting

Hide-n-seek in a corn maze!

Get outside and name all the colors you can find!

Pick flowers and deccrate!

Make a flower press!

Bake a pumpkin pie!

Meet a turkey!

Paint a turkey!

Write a Thank You note to someone.

Say "thank you" to a friend, and mean it!

Fill in the blank. I am so grateful for _____.

Paint a rock!

Paint a pinecone!

Paint an acorn!

Make art with corn on the cob.

Go on a walk with a friend. See the colors, listen to the sounds beneath your feet, and feel the wind on your face.

Ride a bike!

Scavenger hunt!

Plant a seed.

Plant some bulbs!

Stargazing!

Take a deep breath in. Let the cool, fresh air fill your tummy like a balloon. Then blow all the air out through your mouth. Do it nice and slowly.

Go outside and look around.
What are you grateful for today?